BLOOD, SWEAT AND BOND

BEHIND THE SCENES
OF SPECTRE

CURATED BY RANKIN

FOREWORD

MICHAEL G. WILSON
BARBARA BROCCOLI

> THE JAMES BOND FILMS HAVE GRACED CINEMA SCREENS FOR MORE THAN HALF A CENTURY. 'SPECTRE' IS AN ACCUMULATION OF ALL THE TALENT THAT HAS COME BEFORE US.

MICHAEL G. WILSON & BARBARA BROCCOLI, PRODUCERS

Spectre is our fourth film with Daniel Craig and, in many ways, the events that unfold are a culmination of everything that has come before. Daniel reinvented the character of James Bond for the 21st century when he exploded on to the screen in *Casino Royale*. He is an extraordinary actor who has been the beating heart of these films for over a decade. He has provided us with a glimpse into Bond's soul and transformed the cool assassin into a flesh-and-blood hero with a dose of humanity. His commitment to the film series has been wholehearted and resolute. Like the character he portrays, he is relentless in his pursuit of the truth and he always gives everything to achieve excellence.

We are also delighted to be reunited with Sam Mendes. *Skyfall* took the series to the next level and Sam has delivered another exciting and dramatic film — classic Bond with a contemporary twist. Working alongside cinematographer Hoyte van Hoytema, and all our talented heads of department, he has created a visual feast. The greatest example of this is the stunning opening sequence in Mexico City. Everyone in the film crew helped Sam achieve his vision. It was a moment that reminded us all how great it is to work on a Bond film.

We would like to thank all the highly accomplished photographers whose work fills this book. They have captured the film's kinetic energy while providing fascinating insights into the behind-the-scenes action, the wondrous locations and the originality of production designer Dennis Gassner's astounding sets.

The James Bond films have graced cinema screens for more than half a century and no one involved in the making of *Spectre* could have reached such dramatic heights without the contribution of all the filmmakers who have come before us, blazing the trail and pushing James Bond to the upper echelons of event filmmaking. *Spectre* is an accumulation of all this talent, and the stylistic choices that these filmmakers have made.

It is a privilege and an honour to work on this series and we are grateful to everyone who has worked on these films over the years, and especially to those who have made *Spectre*. We hope you enjoy this book and the film it celebrates.

INTRODUCTION

SAM MENDES

Working on a Bond movie is not really a job; it's a way of life. It is a contradiction in many ways — a small family business that is also a multi-million dollar enterprise; a giant happily dysfunctional family that is filled with professionals at the absolute top of their game; a series of movies of immense scope in which you can — if you look hard enough — find opportunities for personal filmmaking.

Fleming's Bond, too, is a contradiction: a self-hating hero; a 'secret' agent whose name and habits are known the world over; an unknowable, dark, mysterious man whom millions of men want as their avatar. Bond is a man entirely of his time (the early '60s, the Cold War, a time of Martinis and cigarettes and fairly dodgy sexual politics) who has become a man who transcends period. He is, as the poet Philip Larkin put it, 'forever crouching under extinction's alp', and yet he has become the centre of the longest-running franchise in the history of movies. It seems we are still interested in the thrill of the chase, masculinity, political intrigue, surveillance, sexual politics, Britishness, great suits, beautiful women… and blowing things up.

My five years directing *Skyfall* and now *Spectre* have been some of the most extraordinary of my life. The places you see in this wonderful book are only some of the amazing sights and experiences that have been afforded me. But nevertheless, here in this book is the feeling of the movie – the heat and dust and life of Mexico City, the majesty of the Austrian Alps, the grandeur of Rome at night, and almost best of all, Rankin's wonderful portraits of many of my chief collaborators. All directors stand on the shoulders of others — and on *Spectre*, that was certainly the case. All of these faces and places make me smile. And, after five years, that's quite an achievement.

Thrilling pre-title sequences are one of the hallmarks of a James Bond movie and the filmmakers set the tone for *Spectre* by thrusting 007 straight into the action during a vibrant Day of the Dead celebration in Mexico City.

James Bond has visited Mexico before – it provided the backdrop to his adventures in *Licence To Kill* – but in *Spectre* the filmmakers bring their own interpretation to the country's best-known festival. According to producer Michael G. Wilson, the Day of the Dead celebration was shot with 'a Bondian style, where everything was magnified.'

Certainly, production designer Dennis Gassner and his team create an unforgettable canvas against which the action plays out, with more than 1,500 beautifully clad extras thronging the city streets.

'We talked about different festivals and processions but the Day of the Dead really suited this story,' says Gassner, 'and though we built all these huge maquettes and puppets, we worked very closely with Mexican experts to make sure that it was all grounded in reality. We are very pleased with how it all looks.'

For director Sam Mendes, who returns following the success of *Skyfall*, the Day of the Dead offers a thematic foretaste of what is to come. 'The celebration of the dead ties in, thematically, with what the movie is about,' he says. 'The film is about Bond being haunted by the figure of a person he thought was long dead.'

Mendes opens *Spectre* with one continuous shot that follows Bond as he tracks an assassin through a Mexican hotel, up an elevator, through different rooms, out onto balconies and across rooftops. 'It was a difficult thing for Sam to pull off,' says Daniel Craig. 'I just made sure that I didn't walk into the furniture,' he adds with a laugh.

Mendes' use of one continuous shot is designed to immerse viewers in the drama of Bond's mission. 'I wanted the audience to be dropped right into the middle of a very specific, very atmospheric and very rich environment,' he says.

'I wanted that combination of sinister and celebratory that you can only get with something like the Day of the Dead. When the film opens, it's almost like the perfect mission and everything is going to plan, but then there's a game-changing moment.'

This moment arrives when Bond triggers an explosive device that destroys the hotel, causing the building that he is on to collapse, floor by floor. The aftermath of the building collapse was filmed in Mexico City, where the art department littered the streets with dust and debris.

The explosion itself was filmed at Pinewood Studios, England, in what special effects supervisor Chris Corbould describes as one of the most intricately engineered rigs he has ever attempted in a Bond movie.

'We built a four-storeyed building and we had a big weight on a track that went down through the ceiling and all the floors collapsed on hydraulics,' he says. 'We worked on it for eight months, and it is probably one of the longest rigs that we have ever designed and certainly one of the most complicated things we have ever done.'

Emerging from the hotel wreckage, Bond continues his pursuit, catching up with his target as he bids to flee in a helicopter. A breath-taking duel then ensues high above Mexico City.

'Everything looks to be going well for Bond,' says Mendes, 'but after the explosion things become considerably more chaotic, and the sequence climaxes with a spectacular fight in an out-of-control helicopter, which is spinning, twisting, corkscrewing, barrel-rolling and plunging all over the place. With the helicopter scene, we really pushed the boundaries. James Bond has never been involved in anything like this before.'

The exterior shots were filmed on location in Mexico City with stuntmen dangling from the spinning chopper high above Zocalo Square. 'It all happens above a square filled with 20,000 people responding to what appears to be an impending crash,' says Mendes. 'It's pretty spectacular and quite a different flavour from the opening to *Skyfall*.'

The helicopter scene's interior shots with the actors were shot at Pinewood where the machine was mounted on a hydraulic gimbal to mimic the movement. Indeed, such is the pulsating atmosphere and heart-pounding tension inherent in these scenes, long-serving producer Barbara Broccoli believes that *Spectre* boasts one of the series' most memorable beginnings.

'The Bond movies have such an extraordinary tradition of awe-inspiring openings and it is difficult to top them,' she says. 'But I think this sequence is so spectacular that it will be up there as one of the greatest pre-title sequences that we have ever done.'

MEXICO

PART OF THE PLEASURE OF AN OPENING
SEQUENCE IS 10 MINUTES OF GRACE
WHERE THE AUDIENCE DOESN'T KNOW
WHAT'S GOING ON. I WANTED TO DROP
RIGHT INTO THE MIDDLE OF A VERY
SPECIFIC, RICH ENVIRONMENT THAT,
LIKE ANY GOOD OPENING, PLANTS
THE SEEDS OF THINGS TO COME.

SAM MENDES, DIRECTOR

FOR THE DANCERS WE MADE WIGS FROM
WOOL TO MAKE THEM LOOK LIKE PEG DOLLS.
THEY HAD AN ENORMOUSLY BOLD SHAPE
WHICH GAVE THEM A PERIOD FEEL.

ZOE TAHIR, HAIR DESIGNER

THERE WERE MUSICIANS, PUPPETEERS AND DIFFERENT PERFORMANCE ACTS SPRINKLED THROUGHOUT. IT WAS VERY IMPORTANT TO SAM THAT BOND WASN'T SIMPLY TRAVELLING THROUGH A CROWD OF PEOPLE. HE WANTED A VERY SPECIFIC SHAPE TO THE BACKGROUND.

MICHAEL LERMAN, FIRST ASSISTANT DIRECTOR

WE PUT THE CAMERA
CRANE ON AN ENORMOUS
TRACK SYSTEM ACROSS
FOUR BUILDINGS. IT MEANT
WE COULD DO THE OPENING
SEQUENCE IN ONE
CONTINUOUS SHOT WITH
THE 50-FOOT TECHNO
CRANE ABLE TO GET DOWN
PARALLEL WITH DANIEL
ON THE ROOFTOP.

CHRIS LOWE, SUPERVISING ART DIRECTOR

WE WERE SO CLOSE TO THE ACTION THAT A SHOCK WAVE RIPPLED THE METAL WALL I WAS TUCKED BEHIND. THE FEELING WAS LIKE BEING IN A WARTIME BOMBING RAID.

STUART WILSON, PRODUCTION SOUND MIXER

THE HELICOPTER WAS FLYING LOW
AND DOING AEROBATIC SPINS, WHICH
ONLY A FEW PILOTS IN THE WORLD
CAN DO. WITH THE GUYS FIGHTING
OUTSIDE THE HELICOPTER, WE NOT
ONLY HAD TO MAKE SURE THEY DIDN'T
DROP DOWN BUT THAT THEY STEERED
CLEAR OF THE ROTORS AS WELL.

GARY POWELL, STUNT COORDINATOR

Following the electrifying pre-title sequence, the *Spectre* storyline starts to expand once Bond returns to London where he is hauled in front of the new head of MI6, M (played by Ralph Fiennes), who was introduced at the end of *Skyfall*. The pair meet in M's Whitehall office, which recalls the domain inhabited by Bernard Lee's M in films from the '60s and '70s.

'In the previous few films we had Judi Dench's M in a more contemporary environment in the MI6 building,' explains Barbara Broccoli. 'But then, of course, it was blown up in *Skyfall* so we had to relocate M. This is a more staid Whitehall interior. It is very appropriate for this film because, as the story goes on, we see Spectre taking on the hallowed halls of Whitehall.'

Ralph Fiennes, for one, loves his character's environment. 'It is a great decision of Sam Mendes,' he says, 'to rebuild exactly the Bernard Lee office from the old designs in the earlier movies. M has a military background and I think the office suggests a sense of tradition.'

The new M appreciates Bond's talent although, as with a number of his predecessors, he is more than a little exasperated by 007's off-piste behaviour. 'We see that Bond is being a bit mutinous and is going his own way,' says Fiennes. 'But M appreciates Bond and he understands the value of operatives working out in the field.'

In M's office Bond not only receives a dressing down for his rogue behaviour in Mexico, but also learns that the Double-O programme is under threat, courtesy of Max Denbigh (Andrew Scott), codename C.

As the head of the Combined Intelligence Service, Denbigh is spearheading a merger between MI5 and MI6. 'He's the new blood in town,' says Scott of his character, 'and he's the face of a new, progressive security service. When the audience meets C, there is a question mark hanging over him.'

Though Denbigh's plans for a new secret service threaten Bond's future, 007 remains undaunted. In fact, *Spectre* reveals a highly focused and energised Bond who drives the narrative forward. Events in *Skyfall* might have challenged him emotionally, but Bond has emerged a stronger man with an even stronger sense of purpose.

'With *Casino Royale* he was entering the Double-O programme,' says Broccoli, 'and then over the subsequent films he has come into his own. In *Spectre*, he realises that there was one person behind all the tragedies and all the encounters he's had and I think this realisation empowers him.'

Daniel Craig agrees. 'By the end of *Skyfall*, Bond is in a really good place,' he says. 'Ralph comes in as a new M and says that they've got a lot of work to do. It feels like a new opportunity to look at things with fresh eyes.'

In order to take advantage of these new opportunities Bond turns to his support team for aid, enlisting the help of Moneypenny (Naomie Harris) and Q (Ben Whishaw) when launching his investigation into the Spectre organisation.

'Trust is a massively important theme in this film,' says Harris. 'There are trust issues with Bond and MI6, and Bond feels that he can only tell this secret that he has unearthed to Moneypenny. He asks her for help because she is the person he trusts the most. She is pulled out of her comfort zone, compromising her career by doing slightly underhand things to help him.'

Q, too, is asked to step outside his comfort zone, disobeying orders in a bid to help Bond launch his mission against Spectre. The audience meets Q in his new working environment, which is very different from his lab in *Skyfall*. 'This film gave us an opportunity for Q's environment to be a little bit different,' says Ben Whishaw.

'It is a little bit like it used to be, the mad professor's den, with all this cool stuff everywhere. It feels very true and yet there is a grandeur to it that I enjoyed very much. I also liked how involved Q is in this film,' he continues. 'All our characters' jobs are under threat and we need to stick with Bond because we know that he'll get to the core of the problem.'

Expanded roles for Q, Moneypenny and M were important considerations for Mendes. 'After introducing the new actors in the last film, there were some real options here as to where we could take their characters,' the director says.

'I wanted to see where we could take them next and that was one of the many reasons for me wanting to do the movie. I didn't want anyone else to tell that story. I wanted to do it.'

LONDON

I THINK WE CAN ALL RELATE TO THE ESSENCE OF 'SPECTRE', HOW MUCH PRIVACY AND INFORMATION SHOULD BE KEPT TO OURSELVES AND HOW MUCH DO WE NEED TO BE PROTECTED. IT'S A BIG QUESTION.

ANDREW SCOTT, MAX DENBIGH

ANDREW SCOTT

MAX DENBIGH

46

DENBIGH CHANGED A GREAT
DEAL AS THE SCRIPT EVOLVED
BUT WE NEEDED SOMEONE
WHO COULD STAND UP
TO M AND WHO COULD
CAPTURE THE COMPLEXITIES
OF THE CHARACTER. HAVING
SEEN HOW CHARISMATIC
ANDREW WAS ON STAGE
HE WAS TOP OF THE LIST.

DEBBIE MCWILLIAMS, CASTING

THERE WAS SO MUCH DETAIL ON
EVERYTHING THAT YOU SEE IN Q'S LAB.
IT IS A COMPLETELY THREE-DIMENSIONAL
ENVIRONMENT THAT HAS BEEN VERY VIVIDLY
IMAGINED. I WANTED TO KEEP PLAYING WITH
ALL THE WONDERFUL OPTICAL EQUIPMENT
YOU SEE ON THE DESK.

BEN WHISHAW, Q

THERE IS AN ATMOSPHERE THAT SAM WANTS TO CREATE IN A ROOM, WHICH GOES BACK TO THE CHARACTERS. WE KNEW WE NEEDED TO GET THIS MAD PROFESSOR THING GOING WITH THE SURVEILLANCE EQUIPMENT.

ANNA PINNOCK, SET DECORATOR

WE'RE INTRODUCING THE AUDIENCE
TO Q'S MECHANICAL WORKSHOP
FOR THE FIRST TIME AND BOND
SEES THE DB5 BEING RECONSTRUCTED.
Q MAKES A JOKE ABOUT HOW BADLY
BOND HAS LOOKED AFTER IT.

SAM MENDES, DIRECTOR

Surprisingly, given his 53-year screen career, James Bond has never before visited Rome. Given the events that unfold in *Spectre*, he won't forget the Italian capital anytime soon. It is in the Eternal City that he meets the stunning Lucia, infiltrates a high-level Spectre meeting chaired by the enigmatic Oberhauser and engages in a breakneck car chase in his Aston Martin DB10.

The Rome sequence opens with 007 watching the funeral of the assassin he dispatched in Mexico City. It is here that he meets the assassin's seductive widow, Lucia, who is played by Monica Bellucci. Producers Michael G. Wilson and Barbara Broccoli had long coveted the actress, bidding to recruit her a number of times across the years. 'We thought she was the one that got away,' says Wilson, 'so we're absolutely delighted she was able to come on board.'

The Italian actress is equally enamoured by her casting. 'It is a little strange to finally be in a Bond film when you are 50 years old,' she says, 'but I think it is interesting because nowadays we have a fresh approach as to how women are seen in movies.'

'It was a special shoot for me and I especially loved the last line that James says to Lucia,' she continues. 'It wasn't in the script; Daniel added it in Italian, whispering, "Buona fortuna, Donna Lucia," which means, "Good fortune, Lady Lucia." It was a beautiful moment.'

Once he has enjoyed his beautiful moment with Lucia, Bond goes in search of the organisation for which her late husband worked. It is a hunt that leads him into the very maw of death;

he penetrates a high-ranking Spectre meeting and comes face to face with an old adversary, Oberhauser.

This character comes to life courtesy of a very special performance from Christoph Waltz. 'He is really chilling in this role and quite brilliant,' says Mendes of Waltz. 'Christoph is so subtle and precise.'

Oberhauser represents another stellar entry in Waltz's canon of memorable screen villains. 'An interesting character always has an interesting past,' says Waltz, 'and that is certainly the case with Oberhauser. There was a lot to work with.' Waltz's character is introduced from the shadows of the Spectre meeting, and the actor notes that the filmmakers designed and constructed an awe-inspiring set on the Pinewood stages.

Spectre meetings have appeared on screen before, perhaps most famously in *Thunderball*, and Mendes and his team had to create something fresh and intimidating, with plenty of grandeur and a sense of scale. 'I was very impressed with the set they built for the Spectre meeting,' Waltz says.

'They created this huge Neapolitan basalt structure at Pinewood and filled it with interesting-looking people. It was a very classic situation, where harmful people meet to decide on terrible things. And the attention to detail was just magnificent.'

The production also spent time on location in Rome, shooting the cemetery sequence among the towering columns of the former Museum of Roman Civilization in the Piazza Giovanni Agnelli. 'It is all about power,' says production designer

Dennis Gassner, 'that was what we were looking for. We found that location in Rome and it stands as probably one of the most powerful places that I have ever seen, architecturally. Rome has a sense of scale that was perfect for this story.'

Rome provides the canvas against which the first of Bond's three showdowns with the Spectre henchman Hinx (Dave Bautista) plays out. Once Oberhauser spots Bond at the meeting, he sends this terrifying killer to bring him in. Bond makes his escape and the duo then race their supercars through the city streets.

Like Aston Martin, Jaguar cars have a history in Bond films and here an Aston DB10 takes on a Jaguar C-X75, the mighty machines duelling at full throttle beneath the street lamps' golden glow.

'Driving that DB10 was amazing,' beams Craig. 'It is a concept car, an amalgamation of lots of different Astons, and you'd think a concept car might drive poorly, but it moved beautifully. We bashed the hell out of those cars and they didn't break down once. We have some eye-wateringly brilliant stunt drivers and they did an amazing job with the chase.'

The high-speed chase is punctured by moments of levity as Bond tries out the DB10's on-board armoury without knowing which switch activates which gadget. 'There is a lightness, wit and mischief in this car chase,' says Sam Mendes, 'which harks back to some of the earlier movies, particularly the early Roger Moore films that have a little bit of fun about them. This film allows some scope for playfulness.'

ROME

BLENHEIM PALACE WAS THE PERFECT LOCATION
TO SHOOT THE EXTERIOR OF THE MEETING. ITS
ARCHITECTURE REFLECTS THE EXTRAORDINARY
POWER OF THE SPECTRE ORGANISATION.

BARBARA BROCCOLI, PRODUCER

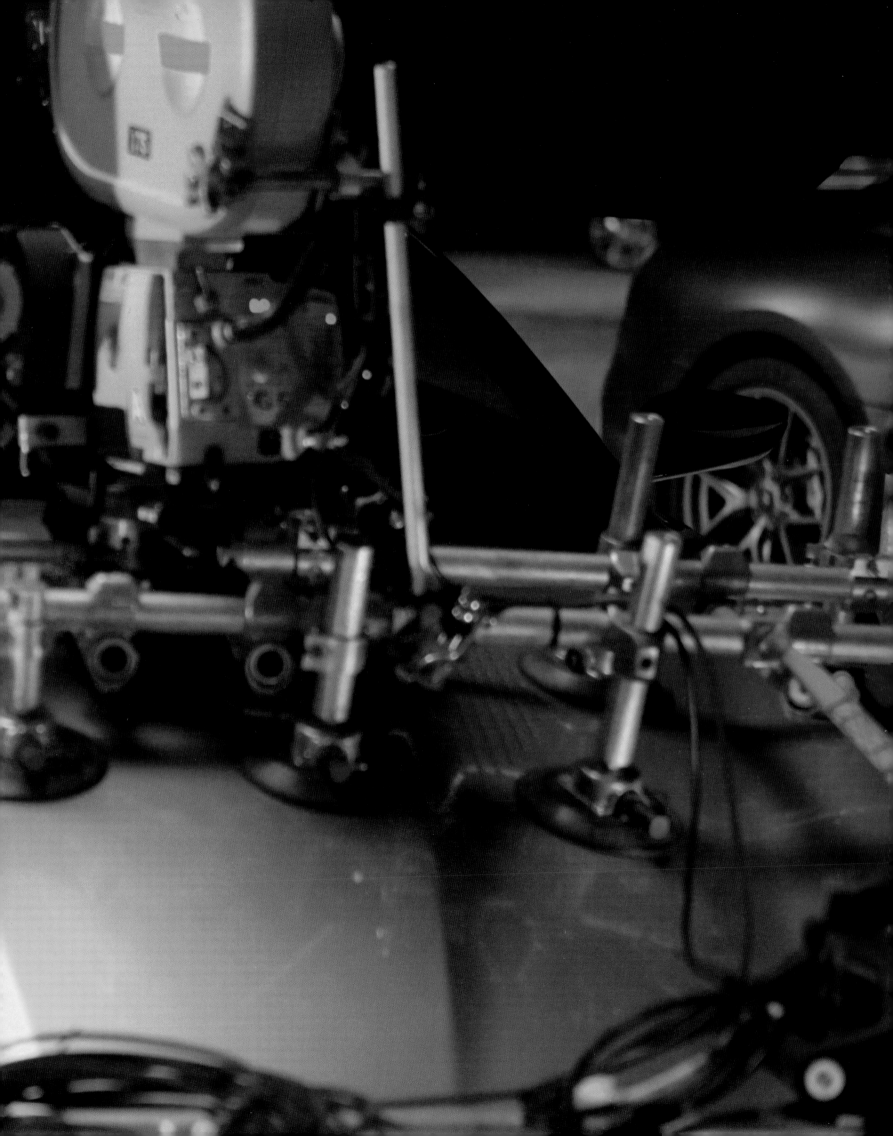

I LOVED THE CAR CHASE BEING A ONE-ON-ONE SPEED BATTLE, A GAME OF CAT AND MOUSE BETWEEN TWO OF THE FASTEST CARS IN THE WORLD, NEITHER OF WHICH HAD EVER BEEN SEEN BEFORE.

SAM MENDES, DIRECTOR

THEY HAD THE CARS RUNNING UP TO 120MPH THROUGH THE TINY COBBLESTONE STREETS SO THERE WERE VERY FEW PLACES TO SAFELY DO YOUR JOB.

JASIN BOLAND, SECOND UNIT STILLS PHOTOGRAPHER

BOND STEALS THE CAR FROM Q'S WORKSHOP WITHOUT REALLY KNOWING WHAT IT DOES. THAT JUST ADDS ANOTHER LITTLE TWIST.

SAM MENDES, DIRECTOR

BOTH VEHICLES WERE KIT CARS SO UNLIKE THE PREVIOUS VANQUISH OR XKR WE COULDN'T JUST GO DOWN TO THE FACTORY AND PULL FIVE GEAR BOXES OFF THE SHELF. EVERYTHING WAS BESPOKE WHICH MADE IT MUCH MORE CHALLENGING.

CHRIS CORBOULD,
SPECIAL EFFECTS SUPERVISOR

While James Bond is no stranger to snowbound landscapes, Daniel Craig's 007 has yet to operate in an icy environment. This allowed the filmmakers to break more new ground in *Spectre*, sending Bond to the snow-capped Austrian Alps in his bid to hunt down the assassin Mr. White.

'We are hard at work in Pinewood for quite long periods of time,' says Craig, 'so it's really great when we get the chance to get out and about. On *Spectre* we not only visit Mexico, Morocco and Rome but also Austria, which was a wonderful location.'

In Austria, Bond appears first at Lake Altaussee as he seeks out Mr. White (Jesper Christensen), who also featured in *Casino Royale* and *Quantum Of Solace*. This in turn leads him to the Hoffler Klinik, an exclusive location for the body and mind, where he meets Mr. White's highly accomplished daughter, Madeleine Swann (Léa Seydoux), a woman who has an important bearing on Bond's future.

'I wanted the audience to find these two, lonely, isolated people — Mr. White and then Madeleine — in a cold, detached, seemingly unemotional environment,' explains Sam Mendes, 'and that suggested a frozen wasteland in the Alps.'

Mendes notes that Madeleine is on her own journey, trying to discover what happened to her father. 'She is not just a pretty girl trotting along beside Bond,' he says. 'She has independence and a drive, which is very attractive. In an hour-and-a-half of movie time she must become a character for

whom Bond would consider leaving everything, and I think Léa pulls that off. She is an amazing actress.'

At first, Madeleine gives Bond the cold shoulder, though eventually they build up a layer of trust and their paths become entwined. 'To begin with, Madeleine gives him hell,' says Barbara Broccoli, 'but as the story progresses we see that she has a profound effect on Bond.'

Actress Léa Seydoux agrees. 'Madeleine comes to understand James in ways that other girls perhaps can't,' she says. 'Because she is the daughter of an assassin, she knows something about what he has to go through and that helps them develop their relationship.'

When introducing Madeleine and Bond at the Hoffler Klinik, the filmmakers chose as a location the glass-encased Ice Q restaurant in Sölden in the Ötztal valley, which is also the location of the cable cars that feature in a scene involving Q.

In *Spectre*, Ben Whishaw's character makes a rare foray out into the field of operations. 'Cable cars are great for a Bond film,' says producer Michael G. Wilson. 'There is nowhere to go once you are on board, so they are good places to create tension.'

There is yet more tension during the main Austria action sequence, which showcases Bond's second duel with Hinx, who kidnaps Madeleine before making his escape in a convoy of Land Rovers. Bond then gives chase in a light aircraft. 'We

again wanted this to be something that audiences have not seen before in a Bond film,' continues Wilson.

A key section of this sequence was filmed in Obertilliach, with the special effects team flying Bond's plane at low altitude over forested hillsides, skimming across the tops of the vehicles on a high wire and smashing through a barn. As the sequence approaches its climax, Bond is forced to land the plane on the snow at high speed, skidding it along on its belly. To execute this stunt, the special effects team came up with an innovative plan.

'We had planes that had powerful skidoos mounted inside the aircrafts' bodies,' explains special effects supervisor Chris Corbould, 'so that once a plane landed it could drive along the ground at high speed.

'It looks as though it is sliding on the snow but actually it is being driven and steered from inside. We also had other planes that we used to do a 400-metre run on high wires at very high speeds as we see Bond fly over the top of the Land Rovers.'

According to the actor who plays Hinx, Dave Bautista, his character loves this high-stakes game of cat and mouse that unfolds with 007. 'In my mind, Hinx is really enjoying this duel,' he says. 'The scene in Austria is very elaborate and dangerous but they've got the world's best people working on this film. The scenes are absolutely beautiful and I got totally immersed in them.'

AUSTRIA

**BOND AND MR. WHITE HAVE
A SERIOUS CONVERSATION ABOUT
LIFE AND LEGACY BY THE LIGHT
OF A SINGLE BULB. IT'S A LEAP
FROM THE WHITENESS AND
OPENNESS OF NATURE INTO
A MORE CLAUSTROPHOBIC WORLD.**

HOYTE VAN HOYTEMA, DIRECTOR OF PHOTOGRAPHY

IT'S SURPRISING HOW SOMETHING AS SIMPLE AS THE SPECTRE RING CAN GO THROUGH SO MANY DESIGN PHASES. WHEN I WAS TALKING TO SAM ABOUT IT HE SAID, 'I LIKE THE RING YOU'RE WEARING.' AND THAT WAS THAT.

BEN WILKINSON, PROP MASTER

THE MOST DIFFICULT ASPECT OF THE SNOWSTORM WAS THE FACT THAT IT OCCURRED SO HIGH UP THE MOUNTAIN, ABOVE 10,000 FEET. THE SHORTNESS OF BREATH CARRYING HEAVY CAMERA BAGS UP THE SLOPES MADE YOU REGRET THAT EXTRA CROISSANT.

JONATHAN OLLEY, STILLS PHOTOGRAPHER

MADELEINE NEEDED TO BE SOULFUL, FEISTY AND COMPLICATED. IT'S A PIVOTAL RELATIONSHIP WITH BOND SO IT COULDN'T HAVE BEEN A TOTAL NEWCOMER, THE CHARACTER NEEDED SOMEONE WITH A CERTAIN AMOUNT OF LIFE EXPERIENCE.

SAM MENDES, DIRECTOR

THE SNOW CONTRIBUTES SOMETHING SINISTER TO THE ATMOSPHERE. YOU FEEL SOMETHING UNSETTLING IS ABOUT TO HAPPEN AND THAT PLAYS WELL FOR THE CABLE CAR SCENE, WHICH IS VERY TENSE.

BEN WHISHAW, Q

BEN WHISHAW

Q

THE CARS HAD TO DRIVE
IN SYNC WITH THE PLANE
WHICH WAS FLYING AT
ABOUT 110MPH. IT WAS
ESPECIALLY DIFFICULT FOR
THE DRIVERS WHO WERE ON
A CURVING DOWNHILL ROAD.

ALEXANDER WITT, SECOND UNIT DIRECTOR

**THE PLANE WAS HANGING ON A HIGH WIRE
DOWN THE VALLEY AND ONCE IT HAD LOST
ITS WINGS WE HAD SKIDOOS INSIDE TO
DRIVE IT DOWN THE MOUNTAIN.**

CHRIS CORBOULD, SPECIAL EFFECTS SUPERVISOR

130

THE BIG ONE WAS THE BARN WHICH
WE BOUGHT, DISMANTLED AND THEN
DROVE ACROSS THE OTHER SIDE OF
AUSTRIA, WHERE WE STRAPPED IT
BACK TOGETHER AGAIN. USING OLD
TIMBERS MEANT IT LOOKED NATURAL
AND WE WEREN'T SPENDING TIME
WITH PAINTERS TRYING TO MATCH
ALL THE WOOD.

CHRIS LOWE, SUPERVISING ART DIRECTOR

After their escapades in Austria bring Bond and Madeleine closer together, they travel to Morocco, each of them in search of their own answers. And it is in the heat of North Africa that their relationship thaws and romance starts to unfold. 'I wanted their relationship to take place in a kind of romantic emptiness,' says Sam Mendes, 'so that suggested the desert and Tangier.'

The Tangier hotel in which the couple stay is the place where Madeleine's father and mother had spent their honeymoon during happier times. 'It had to be romantic,' says production designer Dennis Gassner. 'This is the romantic part of the film and that then carries through to the scenes on board the train.'

Bond and Madeleine make a discovery in the hotel that brings their separate missions together and they embark on a journey deep into Morocco, travelling aboard a train bedecked with vintage carriages. Train journeys figure prominently in the James Bond canon, 'and we can create some wonderful trains that don't really exist,' says producer Michael G. Wilson, 'but that is part of the fantasy of the Bond films; this is a universe where things like that do exist.'

This train journey is layered with romance, although Wilson reveals that the action soon kicks in again. 'Bond films don't let the romance go on too long,' he says. The action sees Bond engage in his third and final duel with Hinx. 'When people think of fights aboard trains they might remember *From Russia With Love*,' says Wilson, recalling the scrap between Sean Connery's Bond and Donald 'Red' Grant, 'but we think that this one is even more spectacular.'

The fight with the hulking henchman Hinx tests Bond's mettle to the full and Madeleine is forced into the action in a bid to help him. 'I loved shooting that scene,' says Léa Seydoux. 'Madeleine is not a super physical character but I have a fight sequence and I did it myself. I have to say I was quite scared but like Madeleine I went beyond my fears.'

Eventually, Bond and Madeleine arrive at the end of the line, disembarking at a desolate station out in the middle of the desert. A car then appears shimmering in the heat and carries them off to what Gassner describes as a 'strange and magical' destination.

This is Oberhauser's lair, a sprawling complex housed inside an enormous crater. 'It is contemporary, slightly futuristic even,' explains Gassner. 'It is an information gathering centre and it's exactly what you'd expect a Bond villain to have. This place gives him access to everything. That is why he is so powerful. Information is power.'

Deep in Spectre territory, Bond faces his sternest test as he and Oberhauser spar verbally, and mentally, a process that exposes a deep connection between the two men. As the narrative powers onwards, however, Bond finds himself in serious trouble. The Morocco sequence then culminates in a major set piece as Oberhauser's lair goes up in flames.

'It is certainly something that I have never seen before,' says special effects chief Chris Corbould who planned and choreographed the explosion. 'I wanted to do a "line of fire" with a string of explosions, as if the whole of Oberhauser's underground system is connected by pipes and the explosion is working its way round the pipes and blowing up each section's storage tanks as it goes. It was hard to top *Skyfall* but we've done it and it is a great way to finish this section of the film.'

The vast explosion was shot on location in Morocco. 'We could have done it in a quarry in Wales,' says Mendes, 'but it would not have been the same as doing it for real in the desert. And we had to do it for real. I am not somebody who enjoys making films in computers. Modern audiences are very sophisticated and can tell the difference between something that is happening for real and something that has been made entirely in a computer.'

For the actors and crew, this meant sweating for days in the heat of the Moroccan sands. 'I was lucky,' laughs Waltz, 'I was only there for half a day but the rest of the production had to work for days in the sweltering heat.' This was quite a challenge, notes Seydoux. 'I had to run through the desert wearing high heels in 50-degree temperatures,' she says. 'Believe me, that is not an easy thing to do!'

MOROCCO

THE MADELEINE CHARACTER IS VERY INTERESTING AND THAT'S DOWN TO THE ACTRESS PLAYING THE ROLE, LÉA SEYDOUX. SHE MADE THE PART WHAT IT IS.

DANIEL CRAIG, JAMES BOND

I REMEMBER BEING SPELLBOUND BY SEAN CONNERY AND THEN BY DANIEL CRAIG. BOND IS JUST DEFINED BY ITS WIT AND ALLURE.

BRIGITTE LACOMBE, CONTRIBUTING PHOTOGRAPHER

I TOLD SAM I COULDN'T
DO A BETTER TUXEDO
THAN 'SKYFALL'. BUT
THEN I THOUGHT MOROCCO
DESERVED THAT COLONIAL
TOUCH, A FEELING OF
'CASABLANCA' WHERE
TIME STOPS AND
EVERYTHING IS SO ICONIC.

JANY TEMIME, COSTUME DESIGNER

MADELEINE IS CHIC AND SEXY, BUT IN A MODERN WAY. I LOVE THE SILK DRESS THAT SHE WEARS ON THE TRAIN. JANY, THE COSTUME DESIGNER, DID SUCH A WONDERFUL JOB.

LÉA SEYDOUX, MADELEINE SWANN

LÉA SEYDOUX

MADELEINE SWANN

**SOMETIMES IT TAKES
A SANDSTORM TO REALISE THAT
THERE'S SOMETHING HEALTHY
WITH NOT HAVING CONTROL
OVER THE ENVIRONMENT.
THE SAND BLOWING BY THE
ABANDONED STATION MADE
THE SUN SOFTER THAN
I IMAGINED AND MADE THE
LOCATION MUCH MORE DRY,
DESOLATE AND BEATEN.**

HOYTE VAN HOYTEMA, DIRECTOR OF PHOTOGRAPHY

REHEARSALS ARE WHERE ALL
THE STORY AND CHARACTER ARE
DISCUSSED. I'VE WORKED WITH SAM
FOR A LONG TIME SO ONCE WE'RE
ON SET, THE FOCUS IS ON DIALOGUE
TWEAKS AND HOW HE ACTUALLY
WANTS TO SHOOT IT.

JAYNE-ANN TENGGREN,
ASSOCIATE PRODUCER / SCRIPT SUPERVISOR

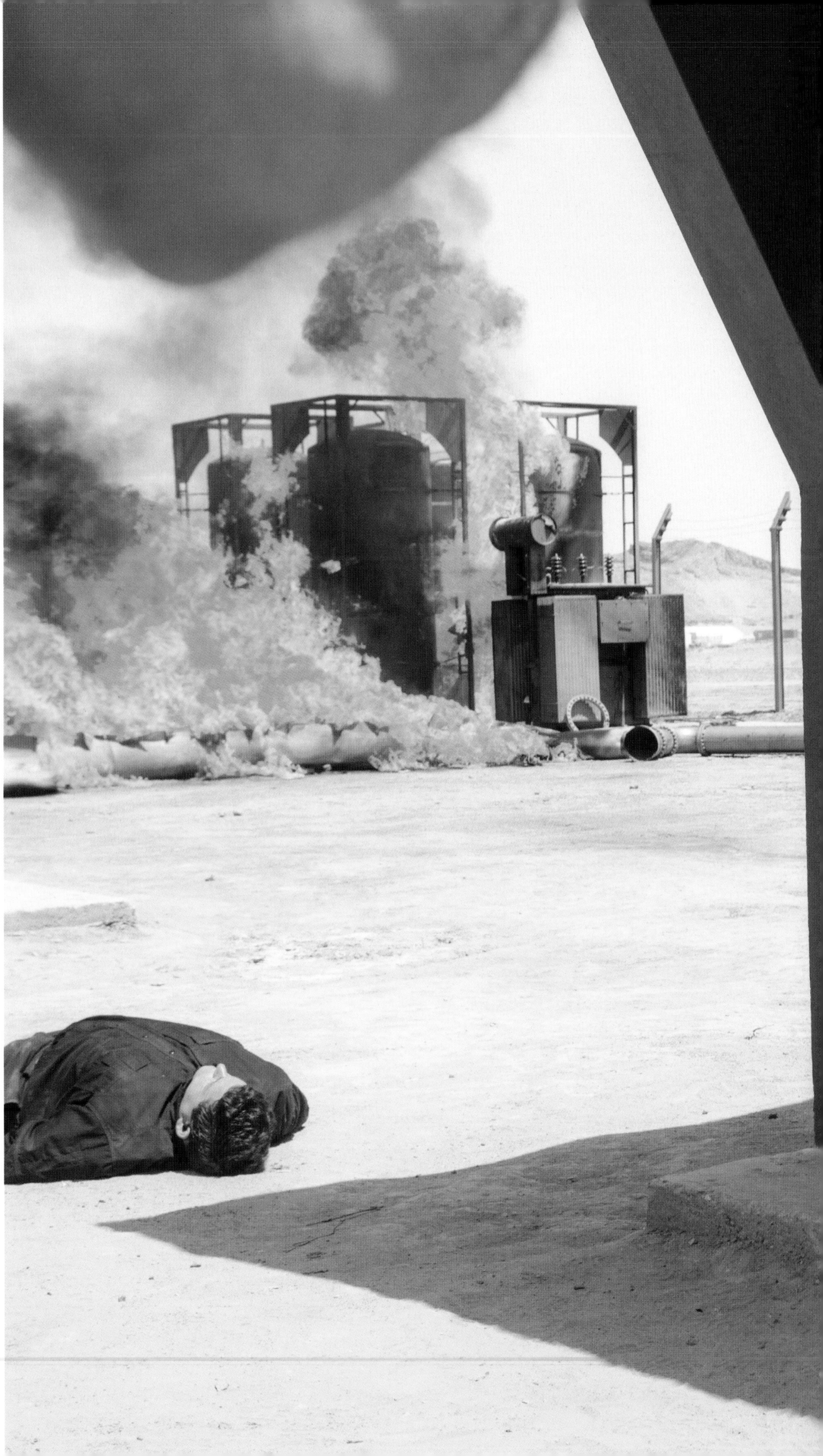

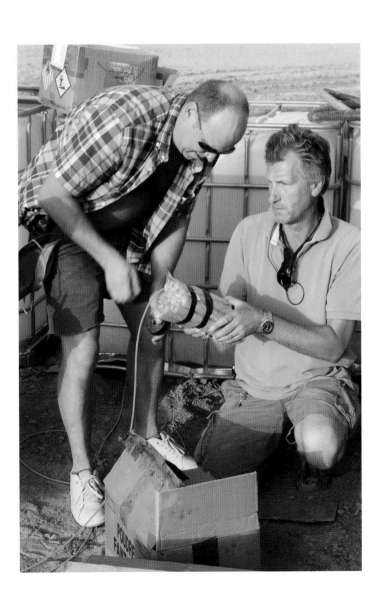

In *Spectre*, Bond must battle a threat from within, as the head of the Combined Intelligence Service, Max Denbigh (aka C), emerges during the course of the film as a dangerous man brimming with malicious intent. Hence, when Bond returns to London after his adventures in Morocco, he engages his support team — Q, M and Moneypenny — in his bid to fight on two fronts. 'It becomes a race against the clock to help Bond on this mission,' says Naomie Harris.

Throughout their history, the James Bond films have reflected the environment and socio-political concerns of the day, and *Spectre* explores this to the full with the filmmakers seizing upon anxieties surrounding the intelligence services, surveillance and the leaks that have exposed high-level interference in the public's democratic rights.

'When Bond was created, MI6 were unquestionably the good guys,' explains Sam Mendes. 'In the Cold War, they were fighting for us against Communism and it was a very simple, black and white situation. Now, the public's perception of the secret services is that they are concealing secrets from us and they are not entirely to be trusted. We try to animate that debate in the movie.'

This is one of the great successes in *Spectre*, says Ralph Fiennes. 'Although he honours the series' extraordinary fight sequences, impossible car chases and high definition villains,' the actor says, 'I think Sam Mendes roots his Bond in something that feels current and real.'

Fiennes' M is called into front-line action during the film's final portion and is pushed into a fight with Andrew Scott's C. 'I did have a bit of a fight with Andrew,' adds Fiennes. 'We did that scene ourselves although often filmmakers flatter the actors into thinking they are doing their own fights, while really the stuntmen do all the real work.'

That said, both men enjoyed their involvement. 'I got to do a stunt on a Bond film and that is really cool,' beams Scott. 'I had to fall backwards from quite a considerable height. I'm not great with heights but I thought I would feel the fear and do it anyway. I really felt like I was in a James Bond film.'

It's not only M who takes to the field in a bid to stop the villains. When Oberhauser arrives in London, Moneypenny and Q are also called into action. 'All of these characters are integral to the climax,' says Ben Whishaw, 'and Q has to do a very important piece of hacking to stop a computer system going online which would threaten everything. It is unusual to see the other characters this involved in a Bond film and we all get to witness Bond's final showdown with Oberhauser.'

This showdown involves speedboats on the River Thames and another thrilling helicopter sequence, which culminates in the villain's chopper crash-landing on London's Westminster Bridge. The crash itself was filmed on a full-size replica section of the bridge that was fabricated on the 007 Stage at Pinewood Studios, although the production did film on location, shutting down the bridge for a series of stunning night shoots.

'I was filming on Westminster Bridge when they closed it down for us and that was really exciting,' says Harris. 'We did quite a lot of night shooting by Big Ben. How often do you get the chance to shut down huge parts of London?

'It was wonderful, and our director of photography [Hoyte Van Hoytema] actually relit these parts of London in such way that the mayor, Boris Johnson, said that Bond should relight all of London because it was so beautiful! The whole film was an amazing experience.'

Daniel Craig agrees. 'I felt energised on this movie,' he says. 'It felt like it was my first time again because Sam was in a great place and I was in a great place with him. We were both encouraging each other and pushing each other. This has been two years in the making from beginning to end, from script to the final part of filming. It has been tough at times. It has been exhausting. But it's the best job in the world.'

LONDON

STEVEN MORRIS

CHRISTOPHER ROSEWAR...

JAMES CORNISH

LAURA FULLER

ARCHIE CAMPBELL-BALDW...

ROBERT JOSE

DANIEL SWINGLER

MARCUS DYE

LAURA GRANT

ANDREW BENNETT

CHRISTOPHER LOWE KBE

MATTHEW JONES

JAMES BOND

RALPH FIENNES

M

WHEN I LEARNED THAT Q, MONEYPENNY
AND M GOT INVOLVED IN THE ACTION AT THE
END OF THE FILM, I WAS DELIGHTED. FOR THIS
M, BEING OUT IN THE FIELD IS VERY MUCH
WITHIN HIS COMFORT ZONE.

RALPH FIENNES, M

OVER THE YEARS WE'VE
HAD ACTION SEQUENCES
TAKE PLACE IN VARIOUS
EXOTIC LOCATIONS,
BUT HAVING OUR LATEST
CLIMACTIC SCENE SET
ON WESTMINSTER BRIDGE,
IN THE SHADOW OF BIG
BEN AND THE HOUSES
OF PARLIAMENT, HAS
TO TOP THEM ALL.

MICHAEL G. WILSON, PRODUCER

CHRISTOPH WALTZ

OBERHAUSER

THIS IMAGE EVOKES IAN
FLEMING'S DESCRIPTION OF
BOND IN 'MOONRAKER', 'HE MUST
PLAY THE ROLE EXPECTED OF HIM.
THE TOUGH MAN OF THE WORLD.
THE SECRET AGENT. THE MAN
WHO WAS ONLY A SILHOUETTE.'

MICHAEL G. WILSON & BARBARA BROCCOLI, PRODUCERS

CREW

Jonathan Olley
Stills Photographer

Jonathan Olley (b.1967) is a documentary and unit-stills photographer based in the UK. He closely followed the team across five countries, capturing all of the main unit photography on *Spectre*.

After leaving the Chelsea School of Art he attended a post-graduate course at The University of Wales of Documentary Photography. Olley's work has been widely exhibited and collected, most notably by San Francisco Museum of Modern Art, (SFMoMA)-California, the Walker Art Centre-Minneapolis, Tate Gallery (Britain & Modern), The Imperial War Museum-London, the ICA (Institute of Contemporary Art)-London and Museo Carrillo Gil-Mexico City. His awards include two first-place prizes from the World Press Photo, a Bronze and Silver award from the Association of Photographers for reporting from the war in Iraq, plus a journey along England's sea-wall and the *Observer*/Hodge Award for photojournalism for an essay made during the siege of Sarajevo '93-'95.

Film director Paul Greengrass employed Olley to document the movie *United 93*. Olley found he could readily apply his experience as a successful photojournalist to the film set and continues to work in the international entertainment business shooting exemplary unit stills and special photography for some of the industry's top directors and producers.

L – R

Lee Smith
Editor

Leslie Lerman
Visual Effects Producer

Emma Pill
Supervising Location Manager

Thomas Newman
Composer

Ben Wilkinson
Prop Master

L – R

Stephen Bohan
Construction Manager

Gary Powell
Stunt Coordinator

Daniel Kleinman
Main Titles

Zoe Tahir
Hair Designer

L – R

Anna Pinnock
Set Decorator

Steve Begg
Visual Effects Supervisor

Stephanie Wenborn
Marketing and Publicity

Robert Wade
Neil Purvis
Writers

CAST AND CREW

CAST

Daniel Craig	James Bond
Christoph Waltz	Oberhauser
Léa Seydoux	Madeleine Swann
Ralph Fiennes	M
Monica Bellucci	Lucia
Ben Whishaw	Q
Naomie Harris	Moneypenny
David Bautista	Hinx
Andrew Scott	Max Denbigh
Rory Kinnear	Tanner
Jesper Christensen	Mr. White

MAIN UNIT

Sam Mendes	Director
Michael G. Wilson	Producer
Barbara Broccoli	Producer
John Logan	Writer
Neal Purvis	Writer
Robert Wade	Writer
Jez Butterworth	Writer
Callum McDougall	Executive Producer / Unit Production Manager
Daniel Craig	Co-Producer
Andrew Noakes	Co-Producer / Financial Controller
David Pope	Co-Producer
Gregg Wilson	Associate Producer
Jayne-Ann Tenggren	Associate Producer / Script Supervisor
Dennis Gassner	Production Designer
Hoyte van Hoytema F.S.F. N.S.C.	Director of Photography
Lee Smith A.C.E.	Editor
Jany Temime	Costume Designer
Gary Powell	Stunt Coordinator
Chris Corbould	Special Effects / Miniature Effects Supervisor
Debbie McWilliams	Casting
Steve Begg	Visual Effects Supervisor
Andrew Whitehurst	Associate Visual Effects Supervisor
Leslie Lerman	Visual Effects Producer
Daniel Kleinman	Main Titles
Thomas Newman	Composer
Angus More Gordon	Unit Production Manager
Janine Modder	Unit Production Manager (UK)
Michael Lerman	First Assistant Director
Lukasz Bielan	Camera Operator
Stuart Wilson	Production Sound Mixer
John Lee	First Assistant Editor
Chris Lowe	Supervising Art Director
Anna Pinnock	Set Decorator
Ben Wilkinson	Prop Master
Joss Skottowe	Supervising Armourer
Stephen Bohan	Construction Manager
Ben Dixon	Key Second Assistant Director
Joey Coughlin	Second Assistant Director
Chloe Chesterton	Second Assistant Director
Naomi Donne	Make-Up Designer
Zoe Tahir	Hair Designer
Donald Mowat	Make-Up Artist to Daniel Craig
Kenny Crouch	Costume Supervisor
David Smith	Gaffer
Gary Hymns	Key Grip
Peter Notley	SFX Floor Supervisor
Stephanie Wenborn	Marketing and Publicity
Heather Callow	Unit Publicist
Jonathan Olley	Stills Photographer
Rosie Moutrie	Digital Publicist
Jenni McMurrie	Promotions
Sean Hill	EPK Cameraman
Stacy Perskie	Co-Producer (Mexico)
Roberto Malerba	Line Producer (Italy)
Dr. Wolfgang Ramml	Line Producer (Austria)
Zak Alaoui	Line Producer (Morocco)
Nick Laws	Production Manager (Mexico)
Nick Fulton	Production Manager (Italy)
Martin Joy	Production Manager (Austria)
James Grant	Production Manager (Morocco)
Hannah Godwin	Production Supervisor
Lulu Morgan	Production Supervisor (Austria)
Michael Solinger	Post Production Supervisor
Bertie Spiegelberg	Production Coordinator
Emma Pill	Supervising Location Manager
Ali James	Location Manager (Mexico)
Duncan Broadfoot	Location Manager (Mexico)
Matt Jones	Location Manager (Italy)
Richard Hill	Location Manager (Italy)
Ben Piltz	Location Manager (Austria)
Charlie Hayes	Location Manager (Morocco)
Finlay Bradbury	Location Manager (UK)
Tom Crooke	Location Manager (UK)

SECOND UNIT

Alexander Witt	Second Unit Director / Director of Photography
Jallo Faber	Director of Photography
Terry Madden	First Assistant Director
George Walker	First Assistant Director (Rome)
Dominic Fysh	First Assistant Director (UK)
Clive Jackson	Camera Operator
Terence Madden	Second Assistant Director
Russell Lodge	Production Manager
Linda Gamble	Publicist
Emma Davie	Publicist
Jasin Boland	Stills Photographer
Ian Lowe	SFX Floor Supervisor
Kate Garbett	Production Supervisor
Samantha Arnold	Production Coordinator

Vêtement

No. 10126

الأطلس، السكك الحديدية المغربية

CHEMINS DE FER DE L'ATLAS AU MAROC

THANKS

SPECIAL THANKS

When you are watching Bond on the screen you see a fantasy. A spectacular world to jump into, battle against and of course fall in love with. What I hadn't fully realised was that this fantasy does exist.

When I first walked on to the sets at Pinewood Studios I was genuinely speechless. Every inch designed, painted and built to such enormity that it still blows my mind. There is no other production like a Bond film; the detail, the heritage and above all the people who make it.

When Michael G. Wilson and Barbara Broccoli asked me to be a part of this project, I wanted to show what it took to produce a monumental film like *Spectre* from the ground up. This book is a celebration of everyone who made it happen and honours each head of department for their immense contributions.

In achieving this I have been fortunate to have two of the best on-set photographers in the world. I am extremely grateful to Jonathan Olley whose wonderful imagery forms the majority of this book, as well as Jasin Boland for his great second unit work. Also, the fantastic photography from Graciela Iturbide, Anderson & Low, Mary McCartney and Brigitte Lacombe who have brought a unique perspective to Bond and added another layer of magic.

This book, and the film, could not have happened without the continued support of Michael and Barbara. I am so grateful to them for asking me to do this, as well as Stephanie Wenborn, Jenni McMurrie, Heather Callow, Rebecca Rae, Isabelle Driscoll and Sophie Butler at EON Productions who have supported my team and I along the way.

Last but by no means least, I want to thank the brilliant cast and crew. In such a crazy schedule you took the time to have your portraits taken by me and brought with you so much fun. It has been an amazing experience to document your hard graft in these mere two hundred pages. The title really says it all.

CREDITS

RANKIN PHOTOGRAPHY

Editor-in-Chief
Rankin

Editors
Freddy White
Calum Crease
Will Lawrence

Lead Writer/Interviews
Will Lawrence

HOD Interviews
Freddy White

Art Direction
Calum Crease

Producer
Emma Turpin

Photography
Rankin
Jonathan Olley
Jasin Boland
François Duhamel
Susie Allnutt
Christopher Raphael
Stephen Vaughan

Contributing Photography
Graciela Iturbide
Mary McCartney
Anderson & Low
Brigitte Lacombe

DORLING KINDERSLEY

Senior Editor
Alastair Dougall

Senior Pre-Production Producer
Marc Staples

Senior Producer
David Appleyard

Managing Editor
Sadie Smith

Managing Art Editor
Ron Stobbart

Art Director
Lisa Lanzarini

Publisher
Julie Ferris

Publishing Director
Simon Beecroft

 Penguin Random House

First American Edition, 2015
Published in the United States by DK Publishing
345 Hudson Street, New York, New York 10014

A Penguin Random House company
10 9 8 7 6 5 4 3 2 1
001-283192-Oct/2015

Published in Great Britain by Dorling Kindersley Limited.
A CIP catalog record for this book is available from the Library of Congress.
ISBN: 978-1-4654-3791-4

DK books are available at special discounts when purchased in bulk for sales promotions, premiums, fund-raising, or educational use. For details, contact: DK Publishing Special Markets, 345 Hudson Street, New York, New York 10014
SpecialSales@dk.com

A WORLD OF IDEAS: **SEE ALL THERE IS TO KNOW**